PUFFIN BOOKS

The Euro Nutty Footy Book

Martin Chatterton was born in Southport, near Liverpool, in 1961. He has worked as a lecturer in graphics at the University of Central Lancashire and has been a freelance illustrator/designer for eleven years. He is presently a partner in a design company called The Point, in Preston and London, and is married with a daughter and a son.

For Sophie, Danny, Michael, Matthew,
Jessica and Zoë

PUFFIN BOOKS

Published by the Penguin Group
Penguin Books Ltd, 27 Wrights Lane, London W8 5TZ, England
Penguin Books USA Inc., 375 Hudson Street, New York, New York 10014, USA
Penguin Books Australia Ltd, Ringwood, Victoria, Australia
Penguin Books Canada Ltd, 10 Alcorn Avenue, Toronto, Ontario, Canada M4V 3B2
Penguin Books (NZ) Ltd, 182–190 Wairau Road, Auckland 10, New Zealand

Penguin Books Ltd, Registered Offices: Harmondsworth, Middlesex, England

First published in Puffin Books 1996
1 3 5 7 9 10 8 6 4 2

Made and printed in England by Clays Ltd, St Ives plc

THE EURO NUTTY FOOTY BOOK

Written and illustrated by

Martin Chatterton

PUFFIN BOOKS

Main Fixtures

E.C.
Rule Book

Away Fixtures... Find the Footy
Greats, Spot the..., Top Tips from the *Scuola del Excellence*, Free Gifts and much, much more!

KICK-OFF

Bonjour, hello and
Willkommen to another slice of football life,
from the team at the NUTTY FOOTY offices. This
time we'll be taking a look at footy from a Euro point of
view. All the regular team are here, together with some
new blood from across the Continent. Due to circumstances
beyond our control (Neil's Mum chucked us out of her spare
bedroom), we've moved to plush new offices in my Aunty
Tut's garden shed. From there, with access to the latest
satellite links and interactive technology (well, Fletcho's
Dad's got Sky Sports and there's an old video game
lying around somewhere), we'll be taking
the lid off European footy-
the NUTTY way!

6

Everyone agrees that British players get better when they spend some time abroad. In some cases (e.g. Mark Hateley) this change is remarkable. In others the difference is hard to see with the naked eye. With student exchanges getting as common as Shane Ritchie (and he is REALLY common), it could be your turn to play in the school version of the Bundesliga, Serie A or, er, whatever it is they call the Spanish or French leagues. To make the most of your chance abroad, follow our specially prepared spin around school footy in Europe.

THE FIRST THING you will realize is that our reputation goes before us. In other words, all foreign kids will expect you to have no ball control, no vision and to welly the ball up the park every time you get a chance. They, on the other hand, will have been born with a football glued to either foot, will have the first touch of Baggio, the pace of Stoichkov and the finishing of Klinsmann. If, like me, you've got the first touch of Tony Adams, the pace of Jan Molby and the finishing of Kylie Minogue, you'll have to fool 'em!

In Italy, as we all suspected,
they only go to school for about
20 minutes per day. This is to
make enough time to do your
hair, eat lots of pasta, ride about
on little scooters, wave your
hands about and say 'ciao' a lot.
Yes, in Italy, STYLE is the
important thing in everything,
football included.

SO, SUNGLASSES ARE VITAL, ON THE PITCH,
even at night.

When playing football NEVER run. Stroll about the pitch with
a bored expression on your face. As you are British, try to
avoid touching the ball, as this will instantly give you away
when it bounces off your shins in an attempt to control it.

Brit kids will feel most at home playing footy in Norway, where the long-ball game is king. No having to pretend you've got a bit of skill here. By Norwegian standards you should be able to convince them you are Ryan Giggs's more skilful brother (or sister). The only problem with Norwegian school life is that they are all 7ft-tall blondes, with the looks of super models. They do, however, have a funny singy-songy-uppy-downy kind of language which is always worth making fun of.

Norwegian PE teachers like kids to be superfit so you'll have to be extra smart to avoid ten-mile runs across the snow at six in the morning. Here are a few handy Norwegian phrases to get you off the hook.

ONE THING that you can be certain of is that PE teachers will be exactly the same wherever you go. To find out why we asked . . .

Professor Pluminthelibrarywiththecandlestick VBM (Very Brainy Man).

Professor: *'I examined over 2,304 PE teachers from Latvia to Luxembourg and discovered that have all been cloned from one particularly vile specimen in the North of England, a Mr Horrocks of Bolton. This bioscope diagram reveals the typical component parts of an average PE teacher: too much spleen, very small brain, lack of sympathy, cold–blooded, big mouth.*

In Germany, to play school footy
you first have to pass a very hard
exam at the Munich Institute of
Advanced Footballing Methodology.
This involves statistical analysis,
gravity theory, quantum midfield
spectrum studies, intra–biological
cardio–vascularic research, hard
sums and diving in the box.

After graduation, school kids spend many hours a
day learning how to win the World Cup and chanting
'Muller, Beckenbauer, Rumenigge, Klinsmann,
Voller, Matthaus . . . Muller, Beckenb . . .'

In Spain, the kids learn how to celebrate scoring a goal before they go on to actually score a goal. As in Italy, style is everything and skill is important. However, unlike Italy, the Spanish don't like defending and this may be where a Brit kid can stand out. If you're biggish, just get picked to play at the back and give the ball some welly whenever it comes near you. Your lack of skill won't be noticed. Better still, become a goalie and learn how to catch crosses. It's a fact that no Spanish keepers can catch crosses. They either wave limply at the ball as it sails overhead or they punch it out (which, as all goalies know, is the coward's way) like some pathetic weedy type.

Finally, always remember our <u>CHECKLIST SURVIVAL GUIDE</u> to foreign school footy :

1. Wear a vest at all times.
2. Take plenty of baked beans. I know it's hard to believe but some countries don't sell them.
3. Even if you speak the language like a native, pretend you don't. This will be very useful in avoiding unpleasantness.
4. Pretend you're related to Damon from Blur. It will have no impact on the footy but you will be very popular with the girls.
5. When in doubt, WELLY IT OUT. They can't shoot if you give it the boot.

Cantona's
Cross Word

Answer the question to find out Eric's favourite ground.
Just put the first letter of each answer in the right tooth.

1. Name the Manchester City forward whose Dad also played for the club: Nicky.........?
2. Leeds United's ground?   **3.** Which English club has won the European Cup most times?   **4.** Arsenal play at which ground?   **5.** Everton's Under-21 International centre half is David..........?   **6.** Which country does Andrei Kanchelskis play for?   **7.** French club — British pop group?   **8.** Galatasaray are from which country?   **9.** .... North End?
10. Liverpool play at which ground?   **11.** Which Scottish team finished bottom of their Champion's League in 1995–6?   **12.** Newcastle manager?

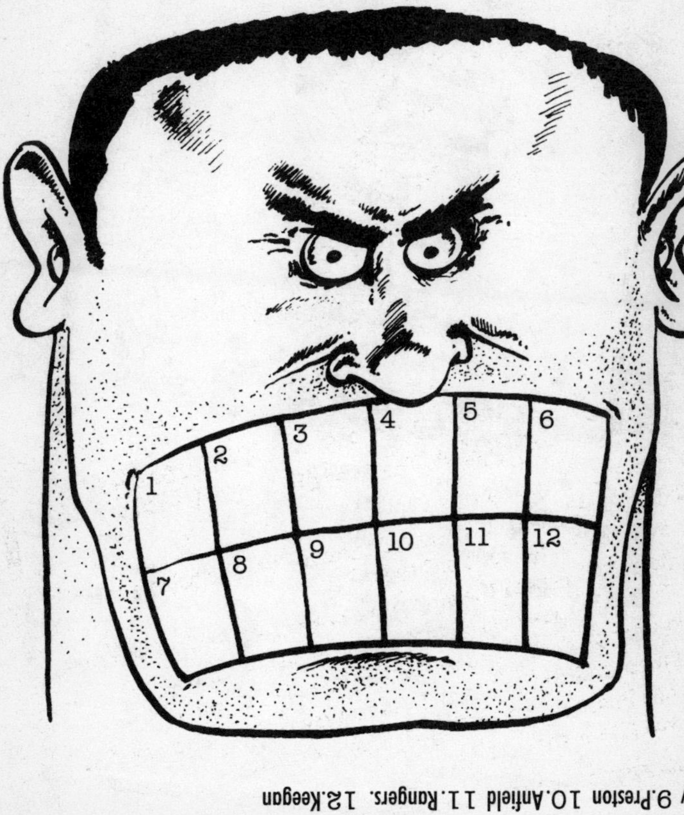

THE EURO NUTTY HALL OF FAME

Clubs: Marseille, AC Milan, Real Madrid, Bayern Munich, Ajax, Hartlepool, Strangeways Prison FC.

The much-travelled Barthes played for most of the greatest teams in Europe before an unlikely modest money move to Hartlepool. A midfield 'general', Barthes seldom touched the ball during the game, preferring to give orders to other players. After a glittering career, things began to turn sour at Ajax when Jean Michel refused to wear his team strip and turned out in full battledress, driving a Chieftain tank. The move to Hartlepool followed, where he fell foul of the law after seizing control of Manchester Town Hall during an away fixture at Stockport.

TOP FOREIGN STARS!

You'd like to play in the BRITISH LEAGUES but you just can't understand the lingo? Don't know your **'WHY–AYES'** from your **'EH–UPS'**? Your **'MONSTER BUNG'** from your **'OLD ONE–TWO'**?

WORRY NO MORE!

OUR TIP TOP TEAM of totally trained translators have come up with this clever little gizmo,

THE MULTI–LINGUA DELUXE FOOTBALL TRANSLATOR*

– that enables any foreign star to INSTANTLY understand **Britspeak!**

*A software power upgrade is required for players transferred to clubs involved with Paul Gascoigne or Kenny Dalglish.

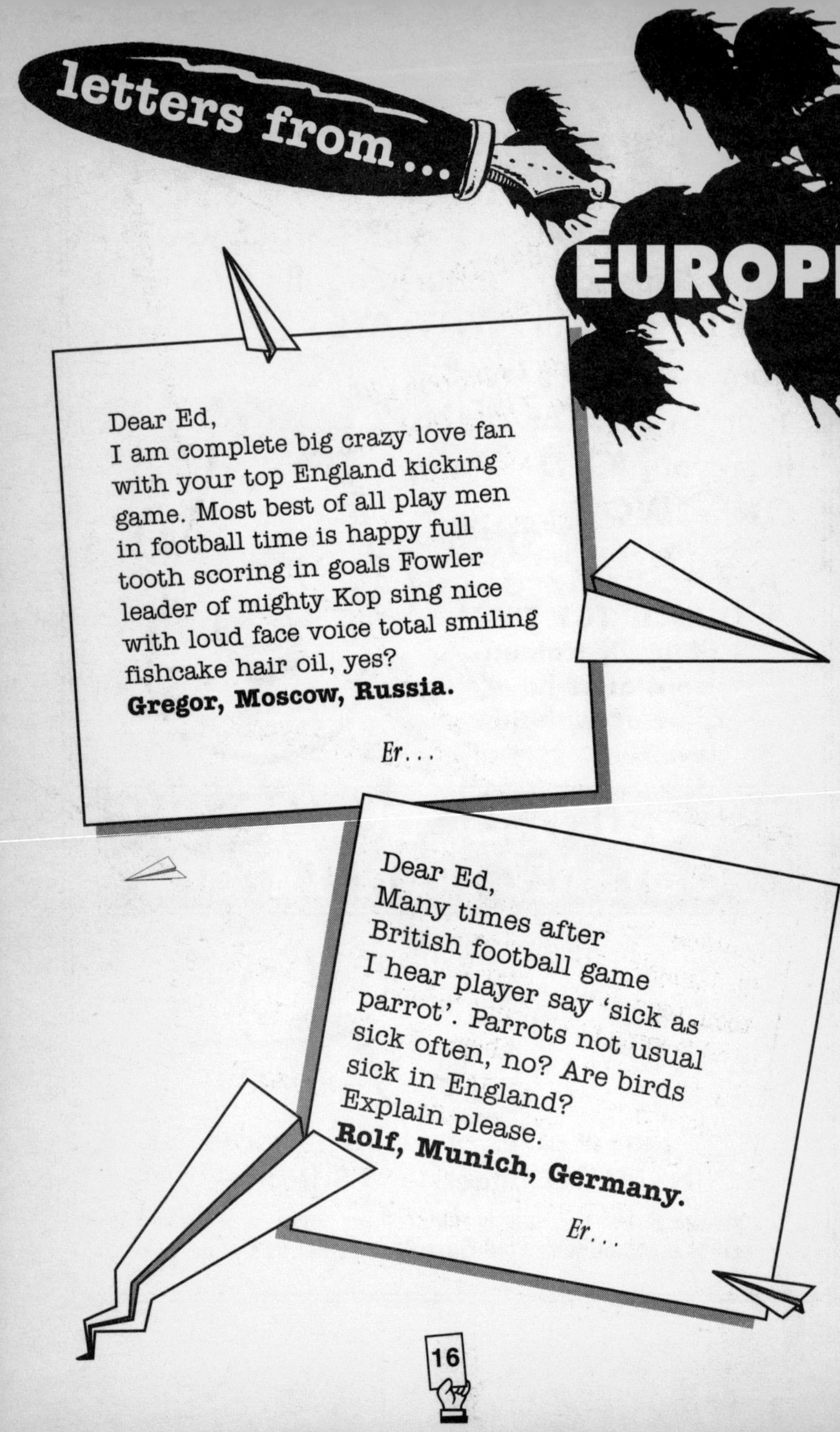
letters from...

EUROP

Dear Ed,
I am complete big crazy love fan
with your top England kicking
game. Most best of all play men
in football time is happy full
tooth scoring in goals Fowler
leader of mighty Kop sing nice
with loud face voice total smiling
fishcake hair oil, yes?
Gregor, Moscow, Russia.

Er...

Dear Ed,
Many times after
British football game
I hear player say 'sick as
parrot'. Parrots not usual
sick often, no? Are birds
sick in England?
Explain please.
Rolf, Munich, Germany.

Er...

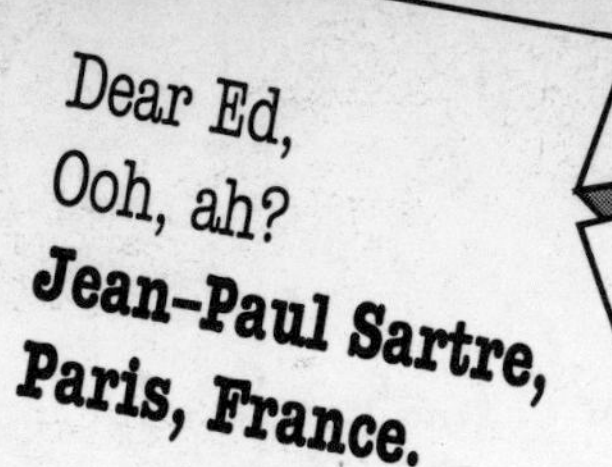

Cantona, I said ooh ah Cantona. I hope that makes everything clear, Jean Paul.

Dear Ed,
Since moving to England I am very confused by a song I hear quite often at St James's Park. It goes like this: 'Toon, toon, toon, let me hear you say why—aye' and is sung to the tune 'Boom, Boom, Boom' by The Outhere Brothers. Can you tell me please what this means?

D. Ginola, Newcastle, England.

Sounds like you need a Multi–Lingua Deluxe Football Translator. Check out the ad on page 15.

Suggsy, the Euro Nutty Director of Football, has put together this handy guide to some tactical masterpieces from across Europe. See if you can persuade your team to adopt one or two of these moves for their next game.

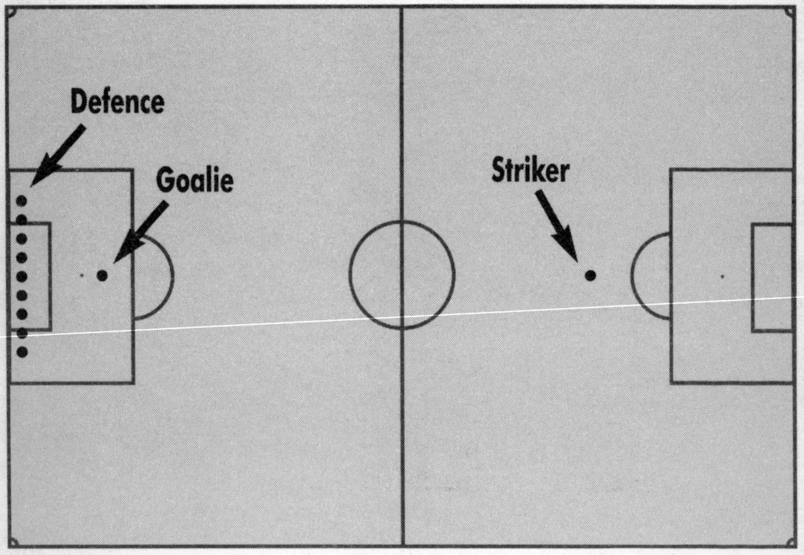

The Alamo

Also known as the 9–1–1 formation, this line–up was perfected by the defensive mastermind Hans Blatter. Blatter, in charge of the team of part–timers from tiny San Marino, grew sick of his side taking a pounding every game. His plan was to line nine players up on the goal line, playing the keeper in front of them and a lone striker (see diagram).

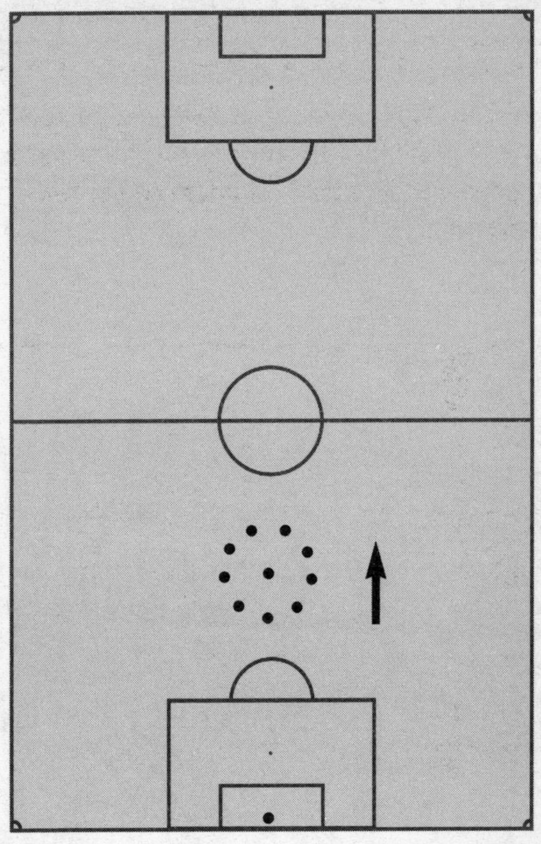

The Wooden Horse Attack

As you can see from the diagram, this Greek tactic depends upon having a well-disciplined team. It works like this: the striker collects the ball and is surrounded by the rest of his team in a tight circle. They advance up the field and simply walk the ball into the net.

Named after the inspirational tactics of the South London Crazy Gang, this formation relies on getting plenty of BIG FELLERS in the side (see page 89 for details). Then, playing six at the back and five up front, you simply play a well–timed L.W.U.T.P. (Long Welly Up The Park) and hope that one of the Big Fellers gets a head, or knee, or anything to the ball.

In the goalmouth scramble the ball might get a lucky rebound and bounce into the net. If that sounds like complete rubbish you're absolutely right.

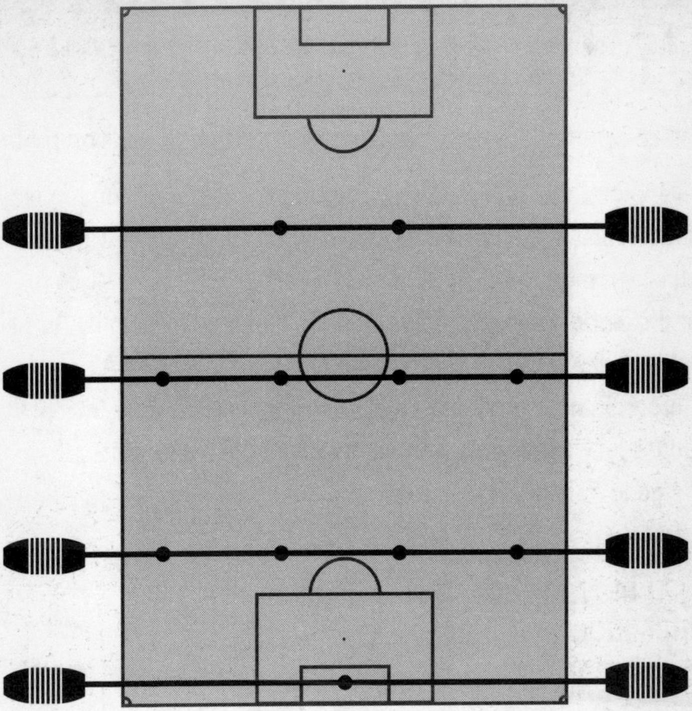

★ The Table ★

Tired of his team not carrying out his instructions EXACTLY as he wanted, Johann Cough, the Barcelona coach, tied his team to long metal bars which he operated from the sidelines. Initially successful, a UEFA ruling in 1978 banned the practice after a number of players fell ill when Johann began spinning them violently to get a better strike.

VIRTUAL REALITY FROM EURO NUTTY FOOTY

Get the complete Euro experience in the comfort of your own home!

At the very forehead of technology, Euro Nutty Footy are proud to present a total revolution in the Interactive–audio–visual–near digital, virtually nutty football experience!

Enter the world–famous San Siro stadium, home of the mighty AC Milan, to experience the authentic atmosphere of a top-flight Serie A game!

This programme is available on CD–Ron (just like CD–Rom, except that it isn't) and is fully compatible with 16 megabytes of a jam sandwich. So, let's go to Italy!

STEP 1: GETTING THE CLOTHES RIGHT.

To Italians, clothes are crucial. Especially in the fashion capital of Europe, Milan. No self-respecting Milan fan would dream of turning up at the San Siro in a dodgy old shellsuit waving an inflatable banana. 'I would sooner eat my own leg,' said a Milan fan we asked. So, the correct togs are important. However, being British, you automatically have no clothes sense so make do by wearing a pair of sunglasses and pouting a lot.

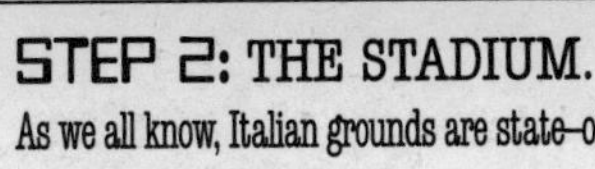

STEP 2: THE STADIUM.

As we all know, Italian grounds are state–of–the–art, high–tech temples of footballing luxury. So most of you will just have to imagine this bit. Obviously our royal readers will have no problem.

STEP 3: THE SEATING.

Although the San Siro is all seating, the Tifosi (Milan's super fans) never sit. Simply stand on a kitchen chair. For added realism invite a friend to stand on it as well.

STEP 4: THE VIEW.

The 15-million-square-metre-banner which is waved before every game covers every person in the stadium. You can simulate these conditions by standing under a large sheet and flapping your arms.

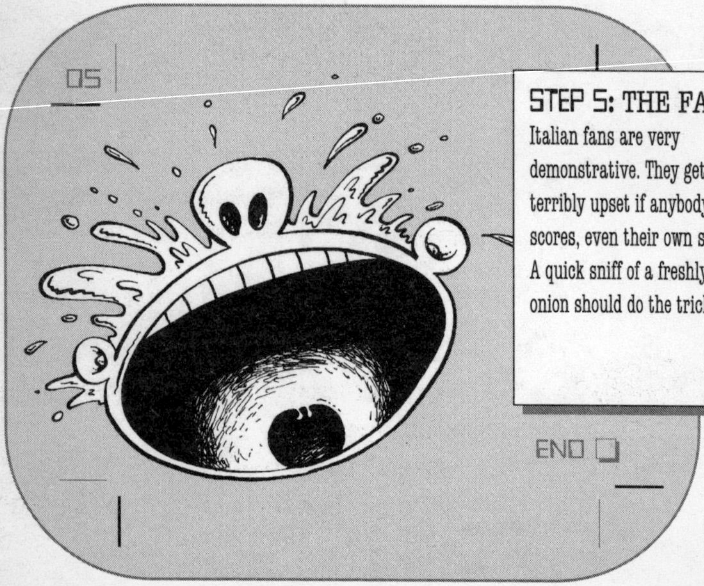

STEP 5: THE FANS.

Italian fans are very demonstrative. They get terribly upset if anybody scores, even their own side. A quick sniff of a freshly sliced onion should do the trick.

A Song For Europe

The Euro Nutty Guide to terrace chants from across the Continent.

Latvia: 'Shmiplo Duplo Plodvid Doop'
(to be sung to the tune of 'You're Not Singing Any More'

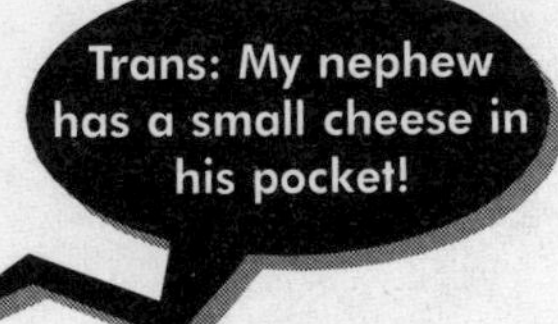

'Shmiplo duplo plodvid doop,
Shmiplo duplo plodvid doop.
Shmiplo duplo,
Shmiplo duplo,
Shmiplo duplo plodvid doop!'

Armenia: 'Uf Slickver Es Um Iggpluff''
(to be sung to the tune of 'The Referee's a ******')

'Uf slickver es um iggpluff,
Uf slickver es um iggpluff.'

England: 'Toon, Toon, Toon' (to be sung to the tune of 'Boom, Boom, Boom' by The Outhere Brothers)

'I said toon, toon, toon,
Let me hear you say "Why–aye",
Why-aye,
Toon, toon, toon,
Let me hear you say "Why–aye",
Why-aye.'

OOOOOh No!

It's the Boring Commentator. . .

THE NUTT
THE NUTT

AFTER-GOAL CELEBRATIONS

Since the last Nutty Footy Book there have been some major new developments in the range of nutty dances that is available to the modern player. Here are just a few of our personal favourites.

No.1 The Crooner

Popularized by Lee Sharpe, this is a fairly simple dance. After scoring, race to the corner flag and pretend it's a microphone. Yes, I know it sounds ridiculous, but give it a try! **Warning!** Make absolutely certain that your goal hasn't been disallowed by a late offside flag, as this dance has an NTF (Nutty Turkey Factor) rating of 102!

No.2 The Klinsmann

Disproving the theory that Germans have no sense of humour, 'The Klinsmann' is simply a headlong dive, arms outstretched, face down on to the grass. Make sure that you give yourself plenty of room for this one. Players have been known to vanish down the tunnel on particularly wet days.

No.3 The Lullaby

First seen being performed by Brazil during the 1994 World Cup, 'The Lullaby' is a formation team effort, involving up to eleven players. After scoring, the scorer runs to the nearest camera (the old guy walking his dog will do if cameras aren't there) and pretends to rock a baby in his arms. Another player joins in, then another, until there is a line of players 'rocking the baby'. Don't ask us.

No.4 The Pooch

Again, this difficult, unusual and rude dance was premièred at the 1994 World Cup, this time by Nigeria. Quite simply, the dance is as follows: score, drop down on all fours, lift leg as if you are a dog and pretend to pee on the opponents' goalpost.

. . . FIFA OFFICIALS have announced the results of their inquiry into after-goal celebrations.

OUT goes running behind the goal and pretending to make a phone call! OUT goes The Lullaby, The Pooch and anything else that could lower the dignity of the game.

However, players can still pull their jersey up over their head and run around waving their arms.

So that's all right then.

Euro Facts #1

The Nutty Truth about European Footy, Straight from the BURRO'S MOUTH.

Footballers often moan about playing 12 men if the referee gives too many decisions against them. In a EUROPEAN CUP WINNERS CUP tie in 1971, **Rangers** must have thought that the Dutch referee had joined the opponents, Sporting Lisbon. With the game all square after extra time, the ref indicated that the teams should take penalties to decide the tie. They did this, with Rangers losing. However, the ref had added up the scores wrongly! **Rangers** had already won the game on away goals. The decision was reversed later and the ref suspended.

At the **Euro Nutty** office the keep-up record for juggling a football is held by me (natch). However, even my keep-up talents are dwarfed by those of JAN SKORKOVSKY, who managed to keep a football up in the air, using only his feet and head, for a complete 26-mile marathon in 1990!

It was a roasting day for the **1995** German division 2 game between ARMENIA BIELEFELD and ZWICKAU. But the game was nearly abandoned due to a waterlogged pitch after a groundsman accidentally turned the water sprinkler system ON! The game was halted for a short time before the cut-off switch was found.

When **Garrison Gunners** play the **Woolpack Wanderers** there's not much local interest as these two teams are the ONLY teams playing in the Isles of Scilly league, the smallest (and scilliest) in Europe!

The Case Of The Goalkeeper's Hair. Keen-eyed footy viewers were surprised to see the BULGARIAN TEAM fielding what looked like a new keeper in the **1994 World Cup** sporting a full head of luxuriant hair. Surely the regular goalie, **BORISLAV MIKHAILOV**, was completely bald? Close inspection revealed that the hairy keeper WAS **Boris** who had had a full hair transplant and had flown his personal hairdresser to the USA!

Marlon Brando, the REAL VALLADOLID striker, knows his football. So much so that he managed to win over £120,000 on the Spanish football pools during the 1993-4 season! REAL VALLADOLID might have preferred Marlon to concentrate on their matches as they finished the season only one place from relegation.

The **Old Trafford** crowd were very used to the sight of goalie Peter Schmeichel running upfield in an attempt to score. They couldn't believe their eyes when he managed to do just that with a final-minute header against **Rotor Volgolrad** in September 1995. It wasn't enough for MANCHESTER UNITED, who lost on the away-goals rule.

THE EURO NUTTY HALL OF FAME

Clubs: Eintracht Frankfurt.

Rottweiler played all his football at Eintracht where he became known as 'Die Machine' (The Machine). Nearly two metres tall and weighing in at 90 kilos, Jurgen was feared across Europe for his strength, stamina and speed. He broke the world 100m sprint record during a training session in 1982 and could eat a BMW in two bites. However, in 1984, in a match against Dortmund during a rainstorm, Jurgen's head caught fire after what looked like a short circuit. An investigation by top boffins revealed that he was in fact an android, developed by evil scientists who planned to take over the Earth. (Have you noticed that evil scientists <u>ALWAYS</u> want to take over the Earth?)

NEW from Kakproducts Ltd the patented HoolyClamp®

Now you can deal with that ANNOYING OIK shouting the odds in the seat next to yours, by applying the **HoolyClamp**®

The fully guaranteed bonded-steel construction renders the idiot totally immobile until you can call a burly lawman to sort him out! Special carbon-fibre noise mufflers ensure peace while the unpleasantness is dealt with.

***Warning:** speed is essential when applying The HoolyClamp. Kakproducts cannot be liable for violent incidents resulting from incorrect use of The HoolyClamp.

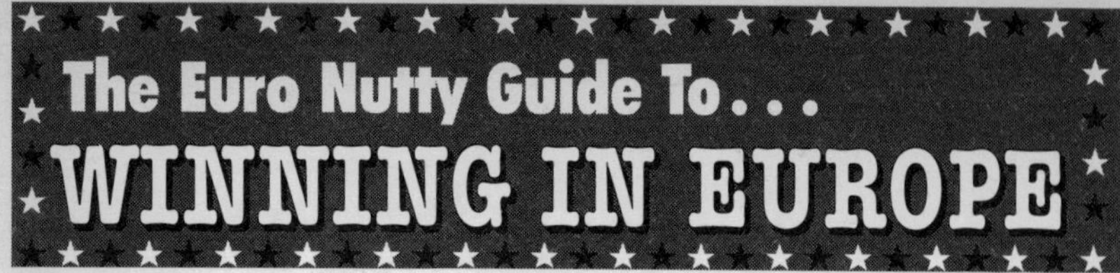

The traditional qualities of British footy – grit, sweat, mud and violence – can all too often seem useless when our boys play in Europe. To help, Euro Nutty has produced this handy guide to surviving those tricky Continental away ties.

THE WAKE-UP CALL.

One notorious tactic, particularly popular in Italy and Spain, is the arrival of a very loud oompah band at the visiting team's hotel at three in the morning. The idea is that by keeping the Brits awake, the local team will easily win.

You could try earplugs, or moving hotels, but we favour the psychological approach. Get all your sleep in during the day, then live it up all night at the nearest club. You may be totally exhausted and lose, but at least you've had a good night out, eh?

THE FOOD.

Since before the dawn of civilisation, before even Sky TV, it has been written that all Brit teams playing anywhere outside the UK must never, ever, in any circumstances, eat the local grub. All teams bring their own cook and, to the amazement of Continental gourmets, chow down on Yorkshire puds, HP sauce, streaky bacon, beans, chips, jam roly-poly and pot noodles.

This is the way of things. Look at what happened to England at the Sweden 1992 Championships: forgot the dependable British nosh and had to make do with Swedish goat liver sandwiches, or whatever vile rubbish they eat in Stockholm. Small wonder we got trounced!

THE HOSTILE CROWDS.

Obviously most Brit footballers are well used to this kind of thing but occasionally you come across something out of the ordinary, like Galatasaray in Turkey, for example. Faced with baying mobs, flares (the firework kind), riot police with guns, screaming commentators and the like, it can be all to easy to play like a complete prannet. The Euro Nutty advice is to carefully cultivate that stiff upper lip. We recommend supergluing a short length of wood inside your gob.*

*(**PLEASE NOTE**: THIS IS A JOKE ITEM AND SHOULD NOT BE ATTEMPTED AT HOME. ARE YOU STUPID OR WHAT?)

TIME WASTING.

There are ten minutes to go and you're winning. There's really only one option, isn't there? Time wasting. We've all seen the great European teams do it by passing the ball to one another. Since not many Brit teams can put two passes together we need alternative time-wasting strategies.

A. The backward throw-in. When taking a throw, simply release the ball on the back swing and send it into the crowd (see diagram) and tell the ref it slipped.

B. Bring on the very tall sub (who is on the bench for just this situation) and get him to balance the ball on his head (see diagram).

C. Get the fat bloke (who is on the bench for just this situation) to sit on the ball (see diagram).

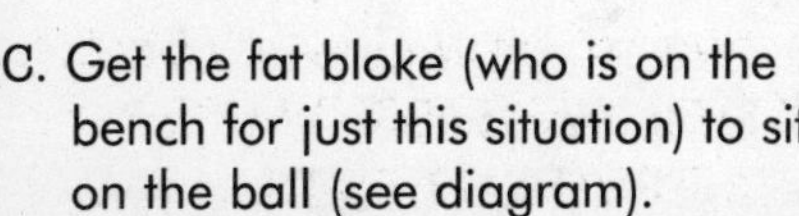

EURO NUTTY NAMES!

If you thought that there were some rather odd names in the British leagues, you'd be right. Sheffield Wednesday (why Wednesday? Why not Sheffield Thursday Afternoon About Three O'Clock FC? Although there is a team called Abergavenny Thursday, playing in the Welsh League), then there's Hamilton Academicals, Partick Thistle, or the much-loved-stars-of-the-milk-ads Accrington Stanley. All completely nutty names I'm sure you'll agree. However, a quick dekko at the European football scene is enough to convince anyone that we are amateurs when it comes to incredibly stupid names!

Let's kick off in the **Faeroe Islands**, the minnows of Europe, whose major contribution so far to the Euro Nutty scene has been the very nutty bobble hat (yes, I did say 'bobble hat') worn by their international goalie.

But take a look at this:
GI, HB, KI, B71, B36, B68, TB, IF LIF, YB. Believe it or not, those are the club names of the entire premier division in the Faeroes. Can you imagine the confusion when IF play LIF? Or the passion that would go into a rousing chorus of 'Come on you mighty B71'? Admittedly the names are shortened versions of the actual names, but things aren't much better when you learn that KI are actually KLAKSYIKAR ÍTROTTARFELAG.

On to **Estonia,** where you can watch Norma play Flora, that's not the two tea ladies, that's actually the nuttily named Flora Tallinn FC and Norma Tallinn FC!

Of course, in **Switzerland** – there are those old Euro Nutty favourites YOUNG BOYS OF BERN (not to be confused with RED BOYS DIFFERDANGE from **Luxembourg**) and the eco-friendly ZURICH GRASSHOPPERS. In **Slovenia**, HIT GORICA is not an instruction but a footy team.

And it's not just the teams who have strange names. What could be nuttier than the first name of the ÍTROTTARFELAG FULGLAFJARDAR (**Faeroe Islands**, where else?) defender ODD ELIASEN? Or the **Belgian** KURT MOONS? Would you be happy playing a WOLF (Stefan Wolf, **Lucerne, Switzerland**) or OLIVIER RAMBO or **Manchester United's** NICKY BUTT? It might be easier against DANNY BLIND of **Ajax**, or ALEX CLOT of **FC Sion, Switzerland.**

Why is it that tip-top, highly trained, top-of-the-range, steely-eyed, lantern-jawed, hard-as-nails footballers turn into complete wobbly softies when it comes to taking crucial penalties?

Why is it that because they can play football, footballers think they can sing?

Why is it that footy commentators always wear those jackets with sheepskin collars?

Why is it that when a football club chairman says, 'The manager has the full support of the board', you somehow don't quite believe him?

Why is it that everyone above the age of 20 thinks that all footy at all times in the 1970s was super and triffic?

Why is it that all England team managers get nicknames involving vegetables?

Why is it that Eric Cantona turns his shirt collar up in that really annoying way?

THE Nutty Experts' view

But plenty to admire surely, Alan? A great deal of effort, with some almost Shakespearian moments. The Nutty attack was busy, always looking for a quick laugh. The joke about Eric Cantona was worth the admission price alone.
Gary, what do you think?
I thought it was all very nice and I agree with Alan and I agree with Jimmy and I agree with you. I used to play for Barcelona, you know.
Thank you. That's all from our experts, now back to the match.
47

Spot the

. . . . Bung

5   6   7

THE EURO NUTTY SCUOLA DEL EXCELLENCE

PLAYING AGAINST THE SWEEPER

The defensive system perfected by the Italians in the
Serie A, has begun to gain popularity here. To overcome
a sweeper, confuse him by going up to him and saying
something like,
'It's all right mate, we're centrally heated.'
As he ponders, you'll be able to get to the
byline and put over a telling cross.

THE EURO NUTTY HALL OF FAME

Clubs: Bari, Torino, Real Madrid.

Gerrfome, the Butcher of Bari, the Terminator of Torino, the, er, Rather Nasty Chap of Real was a fearsome sight for attackers. He played behind his defence, reading the game well, distributing passes with accuracy, and disembowelling any player who had the cheek to get the ball past him. Off the field Gianluca was noted for his kindness to children and small animals. His incredible record of having conceded no goals at all during the 658 appearances he made is spoilt only by the 43 deaths and 312 serious injuries he caused.

OOOOOh No!

It's the Eric Cantona interview...

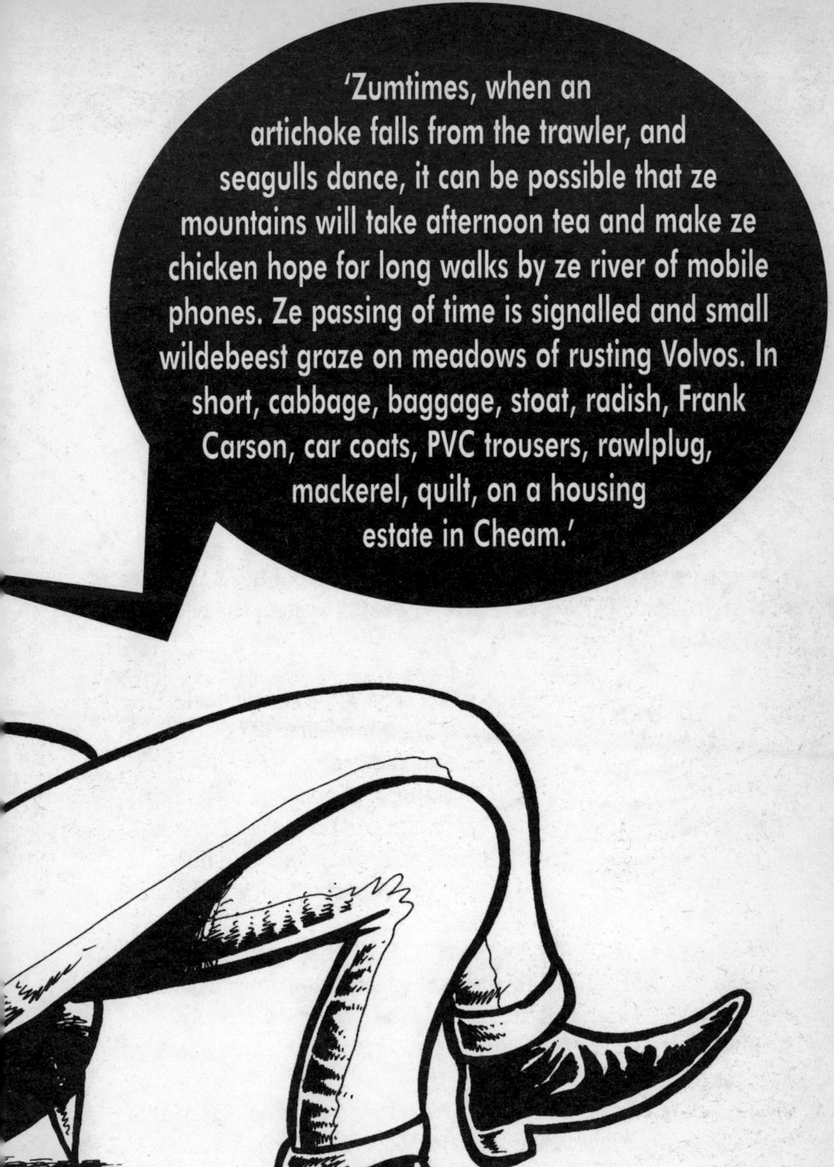

'Zumtimes, when an artichoke falls from the trawler, and seagulls dance, it can be possible that ze mountains will take afternoon tea and make ze chicken hope for long walks by ze river of mobile phones. Ze passing of time is signalled and small wildebeest graze on meadows of rusting Volvos. In short, cabbage, baggage, stoat, radish, Frank Carson, car coats, PVC trousers, rawlplug, mackerel, quilt, on a housing estate in Cheam.'

Equipment Developments In Europe
A Nutty Guide

Most of you will be too young to remember the last great wave of dodgy new bits of footy equipment during the 1970s. Boots, in particular, came in for a number of nutty tweaks and fiddles.

There was the **'Alan Ball'** boot, for example: a perfectly ordinary pair of footy boots except they were WHITE! Just brilliant for those bog-like January pitches.

And there was the **'George Best'**: a boot that laced up at the sides, so that you could perfect those dazzling skills without the problem of laces getting in the way.

My Dad bought the classic **'SwivelToe'** boot. This incredibly dangerous item had its front studs mounted on a rotating disc, enabling the player to turn 'INSTANTLY'. A rash of instant broken ankles saw sales plummet and the **'SwivelToe'** was no more.

In the early 80s there was the era of REALLY dodgy team strips (anyone who ever saw the infamous chocolate-brown Coventry kit can testify to this). Later that decade, only the sight of **John Barnes** turning out in tights (yes, TIGHTS) and gloves when it was a bit nippy kept the nutty flag flying.

Since then there has been little real experimentation. Apart from the ridiculously frilly-looking **'Predator'** boots and the all-black Manchester United away strip we have seen nothing to compare with the crackpot 70s and 80s.

Until now that is.
The Euro Nutty office has taken a peek into the footy future. Read on...

FRANCE

There is nothing the French like better than to set off large-scale nuclear weapons. Inspired by this tradition comes **'Le Bombe'**, a boot which has a 20-kiloton atomic warhead housed in a lead-lined section of the toe. The ball literally EXPLODES off the foot. Direction control can be a problem.

AUSTRIA

Inspired by its Alpine goatherds are these simply marvellous flared leather shorts. Hard-wearing, yet totally daring, these lederhosen make a real statement about your game (you play like a pile of pants perhaps?).

Italy

Refereeing on the Mafia island of Sicily has been getting to be an extremely dangerous profession.

Now, faced with increased player violence, the Sicilian Refereeing Association has produced, after the yellow card and the red card, the **DEATH CARD**. The ultimate punishment, the **Death Card** has proved to be an effective weapon against wayward players.

Take that, Vinnie, Julian. . .

Wales

The idea for this ingenious **Sheep ball** came to amateur player Arfon Griffiths during a match when the opposition were trying to waste time by hoofing it into the next field. Arfon, a local sheepfarmer, installed an electronic receiver in a match ball which, when whistled at, will return to the correct part of the pitch unaided. As a side benefit, the ball is also capable of herding 30 head of hill sheep into a three-sided pen.

Faeroe Islands

From the wintry Faeroes comes the ultimate
in goalkeeping luxury: **centrally heated
goalposts**. Working in exactly
the same way as a domestic
bathroom towel heater,
the heated posts have
been responsible for
cutting the number
of goalkeeping
deaths in the
Faeroes by 20
per cent!

Germany

Now that Jurgen Klinsmann is safely back in Germany and we don't have to pretend we like him, we can bring news of the 'Klin-Gon' boot. Developed by Jurgen's opponents, the **Klin-Gon** has built-in sonic detectors which sound sounds an 'all clear' when Jurgen has left the penalty box.

BENDING THE BALL

There are many ways to bend the ball.
We find that asking a **LARGE BLOKE** to
sit on it usually does the trick.

GREAT MOMENTS IN EURO HISTORY

. . . that didn't happen.

REAL MADRID added the 'REAL' to their name after evil space aliens had cloned the entire Madrid squad in an attempt to take over the planet with fake Spanish football teams. As you can see from a quick look at the Spanish league, this also happened in ZARAGOZA, VALLADOLID and SOCIEDAD.

ALAN HANSEN, giving a summing up of a match, once gave a bit of credit to a forward player and did not use the phrase 'But you've got to say that's really sloppy defending'.

In a 1962 EUROPEAN CUP away tie in Berlin **Arsenal** constructed a defensive wall so solid that it stood for 28 years before being bulldozed by jubilant BERLINERS who had been trapped behind it.

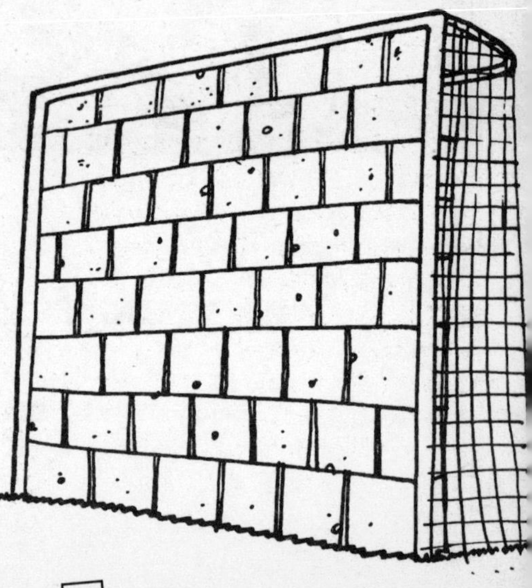

We are all familiar with the
ITALIAN SERIE A LEAGUE and the
magnificent skills of the players. Most of
us also know that the Italian second
division is called SERIE B. But it is a
little known fact that in 1993 a SERIE Z
was formed composed of all the British
players who never made it in SERIE A,
or B. Or C, or D, or. . .

A 1994 climbing expedition had to be
abandoned when it encountered bad weather
establishing a base camp. The team led by Sir
Rudolph de la Beard had been making an
attempt to climb the notoriously difficult North
Face of **Jimmy Hill's** chin.

Anyone who has seen the fantastically nutty
footy film '**Escape To Victory**', in which a
team composed of PELÉ, OSSIE ARDILES,
BOBBY MOORE and, er, SYLVESTER STALLONE
escape from Nazi Germany, knows that it is all
a pile of pants. However, it is a little known
fact that, in the confusion after filming had
finished, SLY STALLONE signed for BAYERN
MUNICH and played 23 games for them in
goal before escaping through a tunnel he
had dug beneath the team bath.

THE EURO NUTTY NIGHTMARE LEAGUE

Let **The Euro Nutty Nightmare League** put you right in the action! Pick a top European side of footy nutters and watch their progress. We've previewed some of the nuttiest players in Britain and some of our favourite Euro nutters. Your job is the hard one - you have to pick your own Nutty Nightmare Eleven!

Here's How To Play

First get a group of friends together before a big European competition starts (e.g. the European Championships or the UEFA Cup).

Each person selects a nutty eleven from a list of all the players taking part in that competition.

You must pick a goalie and ten outfield players (2 full backs, 2 centre backs, 4 midfielders and 2 strikers). Only two players from one particular side can be chosen. This is to prevent people gaining an unfair nutty advantage by picking the entire Wimbledon or Zurich Grasshopper teams. You can then follow your side's progress in The Nutty Nightmare League.

BASIC SCORING

The system divides into two. First, you score **3 points** every time any of your team scores. You lose a point every time your goalie concedes a goal. You get **3 points** for a clean sheet. You lose **1 point** for every booking and 3 for every sending off. So far, so normal . . . here's where it gets nutty.

NUTTY SCORING

2 points for every item of nutty footy kit worn by a member of your team (headbands, gloves, tights, funny coloured boots and so on).

3 points for every really dodgy haircut worn by a member of your side (the definition of 'dodgy' must be agreed on by all Nightmare League players. Disputes will be decided by writing to the Euro Nutty office).

5 points for an own goal.

2 points for a goalie who dribbles past an opponent.

3 points for any goalie who gets into the opponents' area. (As you can see, goalies feature heavily in the Nightmare League. This is because all goalies have a head start in the nuttiness stakes, even sensible ones.)

4 points for a goalie who unsuccessfully dribbles past an opponent (which is much funnier).

Get an additional **5 points** for a goalie who scores (e.g. Peter Schmeichel for Man United v Rotor Volgograd, September 1995).

ADVANCED NUTTY RULES

5 points for a goalie who clowns around during a vital penalty shoot-out.

5 points for any player who balloons a crucial penalty into row 57.

2 points for crashing into the advertising boards.

3 points for running into a cameraman and sending him flying.

5 points for bouncing into the referee.

5 points for ending up in the crowd.

2 points for passing to an opponent who then scores. This counts as a nutty assist.

3 points for missing an absolute sitter.

3 points for having a nasty row with a member of your own team.

Unbelievably Nutty Advanced Rules

2 points for doing any kind of nutty after-goal celebration (see page 28).

1 point for having a silly name (see page 36).

3 points for any player who gets involved with a dog, pigeon or streaker on the pitch.

10 points for any player who streaks.

15 points if a player is prevented from scoring by a nutter running onto the pitch to kick the ball, or by the crossbar breaking or by aliens landing inside the 18-yard box.

There are no transfers or substitutes allowed and you are responsible for scoring your own cards. So, obviously it's really easy to cheat.

NEW

New for this season from
FlikkyFooty!

Bring your **FlikkyFooty** team up to date with these essential additions!

The Cantona

The Klinsmann

The Grobellaar

The Juninho

And of course lots of **NEW** colours for those **22** *kit changes* over the course of the season.

Can be used **INDIVIDUALLY** for team shirt or to paint your goalie's shirt.

DID THEY REALLY SAY THAT?

Here at the Euro Nutty office we're always on the lookout for the stupid things that commentators say about football. Here are a few of our favourites. . .

'*Magnifique, Eric.*'

Elton Welsby

'Oh, do you speak French?'

Eric Cantona

'*Non.*'

'He has always played for Inter Milan, whilst his brother plays just across the city at AC Milan, who of course share the same stadium.'

Chris Waddle

Brian Moore

'*It wouldn't be a surprise to see Marseille play a rough game, but it would be surprising if they did.*'

'Haji has been probably the best player on the field without any question.'

'Gullit. . .turned to find he had someone standing on his toes.'

John Motson

Bobby Charlton

Alan Parry

George Hamilton

Brian Moore

David Francie

John Motson

Peter Jones

Ray Wilkins

LONG MEMORY

THE DUST UP IN DÜSSELDORF

'It were just before the war when, by sheer grit, pluck, elbow grease and a bit of spit 'n' polish, **ASHPIT VILLA** made it through all 95 preliminary qualifying rounds of the **European Cup**. We'd won the league the previous season; the **Northern Slagheap Sunday League**, that is. In those days there were none of these namby-pamby ideas about resting on your laurels! No, us ASHPITONIANS rolled our hairy Northern shirt sleeves up and qualified for Europe.'

'We got lucky in the first two rounds proper with easy games; away to Rangers and then home to FUNNY BOYS OF GENEVA. But in round three came a real test! Away to the Cup favourites, **Racing Nutmeg of Düsseldorf**. They were on a run of 27 European Cup wins and looked set to make it 28. The Nutmeg side was packed with household names, like FRANZ TESCO, OTTO PERSIL and the tricky left wing wizard DIETER MARSBAR.'

| FRANZ TESCO | OTTO PERSIL | DIETER MARSBAR |

'The game was played in a white hot cauldron of sound and fury. Tackles were going in so high they were interfering with air traffic over DÜSSELDORF.'

'I was up against **Hans "The Professor" Audiquattro,**
the midfield genius. He didn't actually
play, he just sat in the stands
thinking about the game.
His brainwaves were so
powerful that they were
able to kick the ball and
move the other players!'

'Any road, after ten minutes of that shenanigans I'd had enough.
I came up with a daring plan. Racing from the
field I rummaged through our trainer's kit
bag. Finding his EMERGENCY
SCALPEL, I swiftly performed
FRONTAL LOBOTOMIES on all our lads, rendering them totally
resistant to the wiles of **PROFESSOR AUDIQUATTRO!** '

'Unfortunately, the lack of proper
medical training meant that I had
in fact killed NOBBY, GEORGE and
all the rest of the team. It were
down to me to win the
game! I floated
an inch-perfect
pass to meself on
the wing and th. . .'

VOODOO REF!

FED-UP with terrible refereeing decisions? BRASSED OFF with a booking?

Finely crafted by **top Haitian** voodoo priests, the **VOODOO REF** can be modelled on the referee of your choice! Made of authentic **'dung wax'**, the **VOODOO REF** allows you to get your own back without leaving the comfort of your armchair.

A RANGE OF ACCESSORIES IS AVAILABLE TO SUIT WHATEVER VILE **PUNISHMENT** YOU HAVE IN MIND!

Gazza's Grin

Answer the questions and put the first letter of each answer in the right tooth to find out what Gazza's shouting about.

1. What top Dutch team has the same name as a floor cleaner?
2. Where was the '94 World Cup final staged, New York or Pasadena?
3. Who scored a goal with the 'Hand of God'?

4. Which current premiership manager holds the record for scoring the fastest England international goal?

5. With what club did David Ginola win a League Championship in 1994?

6. Which Swede scored five in the 1994 World Cup?

7. Which country did Jack Charlton play for?

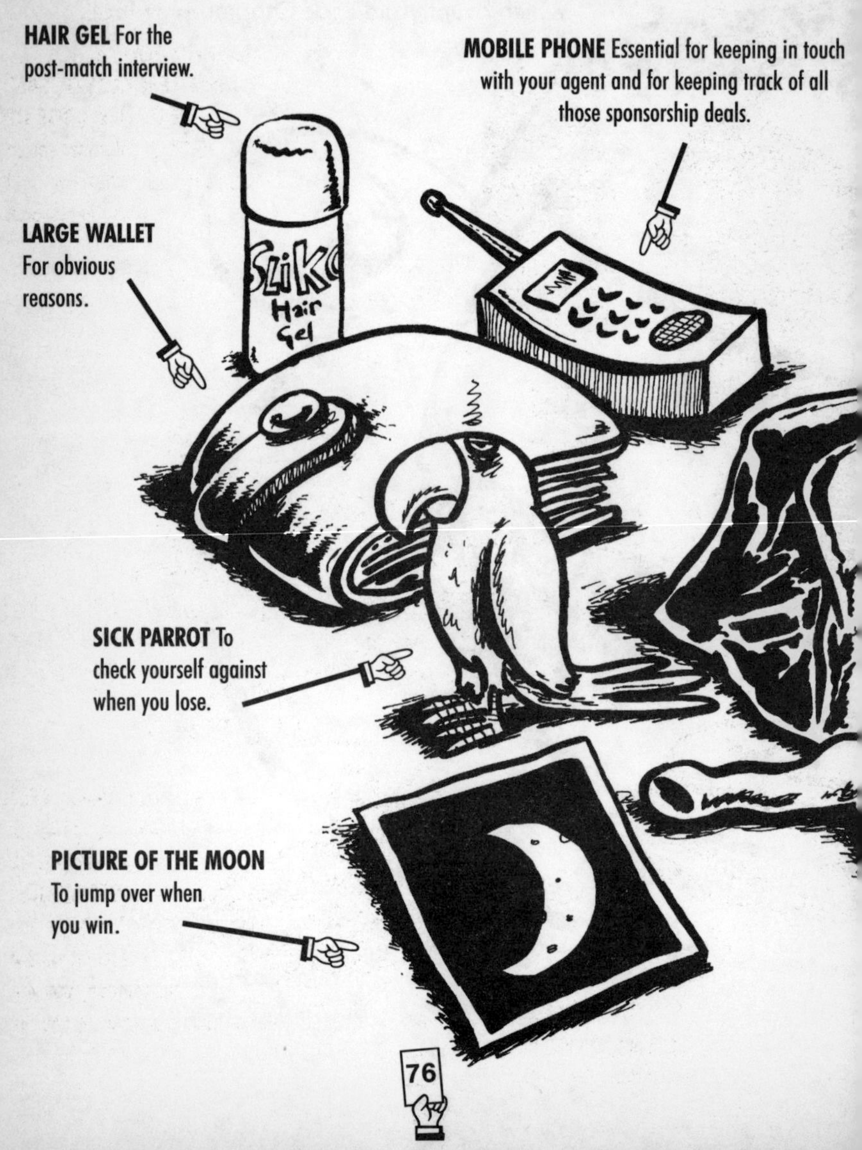
It's the day of the big final and the star players arrive on the luxury coach at the stadium. They step off, each holding a kitbag. Just what do the top stars keep in that bag? Euro Nutty Footy has taken a quick look

. . .INSIDE THE KITBAG!

HAIR GEL For the post-match interview.

LARGE WALLET For obvious reasons.

MOBILE PHONE Essential for keeping in touch with your agent and for keeping track of all those sponsorship deals.

Slik Hair Gel

SICK PARROT To check yourself against when you lose.

PICTURE OF THE MOON To jump over when you win.

76

PERSONAL HAIRDRESSER (see 'The Case Of The Goalkeeper's Hair,' page 33)

PERSONAL HYPNOTIST

RABBIT'S FOOT, BLACK CAT, FOUR-LEAF CLOVER, SALT, EYE OF NEWT, TOE OF FROG It's not that you're superstitious but, hey, you can't be too careful.

TITANIUM-REINFORCED SHINPADS Essential for matches involving 'The Hard Men of Europe'.

Personalized, hand-tooled pigskin, laser-powered, heat-seeking 'IL CARNIVORE' BOOTS. You don't like them but the company pay you three zillion a year to say you do.

NICE SWEATER In case you get invited on to 'A Question Of Sport'.

77

OOOOOh No!

IT'S ANDY GRAY AND HIS COMPUTER ANALYSIS...

'So what ah've done, Rob, is to take that Shearer goal and feed it through ma various bits and bobs of kit ah've got lying around the studio. And ah've come up with some pretty interesting stuff; just watch the monitor and ye can see that, if we cross-reference Shearer's run with the Earth's gravitational pull, the barometric pressure readout and the Norwegian high tide charts, he is clearly offside when Batty plays the through ball. Now, by adding colour traces to the image we can see that the shot travelled 32.654 metres (that's the blue line), it was moving at a fair few knots as well, 67.403 miles per hour to be exact. It took a nasty bobble just before Schmeichel dived. The geological interface output transponder tells me it bobbled on a wee patch of glutinous, semi-liquidized, variegated, molecularly bonded minerals. That's "mud" to the less technically minded. The integral, multi-read body monitors show that big Alan had a pulse rate of 92 when the ball was struck, increasing to 98 as it hit the onion bag. Ah'd say he got quite a kick from that ball flying in! His alpha-wave brain scan backs this up and...'

Euro Facts #2

The Nutty Truth about European Footy, Straight from the BURRO'S MOUTH

SCOTLAND have qualified for eight World Cup finals but have only played in seven! The nutty reason is that in **1950**, when two British international sides could qualify the **Scottish FA** made a boast that if they didn't beat ENGLAND in the final qualifier they wouldn't make the trip to BRAZIL. They lost and, although they had still qualified, refused to go!

The sexy Spanish crooner **JULIO IGLESIAS** might never have turned to a career in singing had his promising goalkeeping career with mighty **REAL MADRID** not been ended by a car crash!

Before the mighty **KEVIN KEEGAN** became one of the greatest European players, he worked at Peglers Brass Works in **DONCASTER**, where he struggled for two seasons to get into the firm's first team!

All change please! In a game at Lazio in **1992** Sampdoria played the first half in their white away strip and, following instructions from the referee, changed into blue for the second half!

As we have seen, footballers frequently start out working in unusual jobs. **KAROL WOJTYLA**, a Polish goalkeeper, left football and ended up with arguably the world's most unusual job: he became **Pope John Paul II**!

In a **1994** WORLD CUP game there was a nutty substitution made during the game between **Bulgaria** and **Mexico** when the goalposts had to be changed after collapsing!

It's unusual for a goalkeeper to score with a long clearance, but it does happen. What was unusual about the goal that ALAN PATERSON, goalie with Irish club Glentoran, scored against Linfield's GEORGE DUNLOP was that it was the second time Dunlop had conceded this kind of goal in two seasons!

In **1993** the FA Cup Final at Wembley finished a draw. Arsenal's **STEVE MORROW** still picked up a medal: his COCA-COLA CUP medal, which he had been unable to collect originally thanks to being brutally injured by his own team celebrating the COCA-COLA CUP victory!

The record for the quickest international goal ever scored is just **8 seconds**. It's particularly painful for England supporters as it was scored against England by tiny, tiny, tiny SAN MARINO, a team of international part timers!

Manchester United's European Cup-winning goalie ALEX STEPNEY once sustained a nasty injury: he dislocated his jaw shouting at his defence!

Sick and tired of watching England grind out another mind-numbing draw against Slovenia or San Marino? Well, we can't do anything about the result, but with our great free gift at least it will look better!

Simply follow our instructions and watch every England game through rose-tinted glasses!

Cut out this page and glue onto
thin cardboard. Cut out the
glasses shape carefully and fold
the arms back. Colour in the
eye pieces with pink felt tip.

THE EURO NUTTY SCUOLA DEL EXCELLENCE

TRAPPING THE BALL

The standard ways of trapping a moving ball are to cushion the impact on a chest, thigh or foot. This always leaves room for mistakes to occur. The preferred Euro Nutty method is to dig a pit, cover it, then lure in the ball (see diagram).

THE EURO NUTTY HALL OF FAME

Clubs: AC Milan, Sampdoria, AC Milan, Sampdoria, AC Milan.

The dreadlocked- centre forward was European player of the year three times. It would have been four, but Van Shtimpers was in a bit of a shtrop about the colour of the trophy and refused to accept it. 'It's quite simple,' he said. 'I just don't look good with silver and bronze.' He also sensationally walked off the pitch during the World Cup final because he felt that the manager was fidgeting too much. 'I need completely fidget-free support from the manager if I'm to play at my peak,' he told reporters. Dirk is now in his third stint at Milan. He moved to Milan again last year because the grass at Sampdoria wasn't green enough, then back to Sampdoria due to 'an over-high greenness level' in the pitch at the San Siro.

THE REALLY TRICKY EURO NUTTY QUIZ

Can you score in our horribly hard quiz? Our team of top trivia types have been trawling the footy encyclopaedias for this collection of nasty questions!

1 Which two famous **Italian** teams share the OLIMPICO STADIUM?

2 Which tiny WELSH CLUB took part in the 1993–4 **European Champions Cup**?

3 How many times have LIVERPOOL won the **European Super Cup**?

4 The **Golden Boot award** is given to the leading goalscorer in Europe. In the 1994 awards ANDY COLE only came second, with 34 goals. Who won?

5 Ouch! Which German keeper broke his neck in an **FA Cup Final** playing for MANCHESTER CITY during the 1950s?

5. Bert Trautmann 6. Finland 7. Benfica of Portugal 8. Atalanta 9. Malta 10. 1

In which country would you find a team called JAZZ FC? **Clue**: they're pretty good finishers.

THE STADIUM OF LIGHT is the largest ground in **Europe**, with a capacity of over 120,000. Which team plays there?

7

8

In the **Italian Serie A league**, two teams play in black and blue stripes with black shorts. INTER MILAN are one, who is the other?

9

In which country do HIBERNIANS play ST GEORGE'S? **Clue**: it's not Scotland, Ireland or Wales.

How many games did JOHN TOSHACK manage **Wales** for?

10

Answers:
1. Lazio and Roma 2. Cwmbran Town 3. 1 4. David Taylor, who plays for the Welsh club Porthmadog!

COPING WITH DEAD–BALL SITUATIONS

It's always upsetting when a favourite ball dies on you.
You can contact the Euro Nutty Helpline on
Freephone 0009898765676545343223547689
for confidential grief counselling
and ball bereavement advice.
And remember, luvvies,
time is a great healer.

BRUSSELS SPROUTS

We've all heard about those European Parliament bureocr, burowcra, busybodies telling us Brits not to eat black pudding, doing away with the pint of milk, and making us eat pizza (well, OK they don't exactly make us eat it, but you get the general idea).

Now, **Euro Nutty** has been given a sneak preview of a shocking batch of changes aimed at British football. The orders, contained in an **EC** document to be made law tomorrow, are an effort to make British football conform to **European regulations** and will alter civilization as we know it. Read on. . .

'The Long Hoof Up The Park'

Henceforth, British footballers are forbidden from wellying the ball up the park without any idea who, or where, it's going to. From now on, the ball must be played by an irritatingly stylish short pass to a well-placed fellow player, and from there moved up the field by means of nifty little one-twos in a proper European manner.

European Directive 1328 (d/19) paragraph 6:

'The Half-Time Pie'

It has been brought to our attention that the British tradition of eating a soggy meat pie at half-time is unEuropean. The recipe, which requires the use of old British donkey flesh, means that European donkey floggers don't get a look in. Besides which, the pies are simply horrible. As from the start of the next season, only croissants, l'escargot, bratwurst, schnitzel, linguini and paella may be served from the greasy spoons of Britain.

'The Big Feller'

The British tradition of playing a large, ugly Big Feller up front (sometimes referred to as 'an old-fashioned bustling centre forward') with two left feet and a head like a rock is deeply unEuropean. Other EC member countries with a more vertically challenged population of 'SF's ('Small Fellers') cannot always field a Big Feller. Not that, apart from Sweden, they'd want to. And, of course, it does get embarrassing watching a British Big Feller lumbering around the Bernabéu stadium after their big money transfer to Barcelona.

European Directive 3428760000 (z/765) paragraph 4:

'The FA Cup Draw'

Our senior medical consultant has warned us that there could be grave health problems for the British footy-loving population who tune in to the FA Cup draw. If they are exposed many more times to the extreme levels of misery and boredom brought on by watching Graham Kelly, Bert Millichip and The Bloke Who Holds The Bag grind out another excitement-free experience, entire areas of the UK could go into deep trauma. It must cease.

THE FINAL WHISTLE

Des:
Well, an incident-packed 90 pages, plus three pages of injury time. But now for our experts. Alan?

Alan:
Yes, but from a defender's point of view the writing was sloppy, the sentence construction looked like it needed some hard work on the training ground and I've read better jokes inside Christmas crackers. I've pinpointed two moments in particular when the Nutty team took their eye off the ball; here on page 11 and again on page 21. That's just poor.

Jimmy:
But plenty to acheive surely, Alan? A great deal of effort, with some almost Shakespearian moments. The Nutty attack was busy, always looking for a quick laugh. The joke about Eric Cantona was worth the admission price alone.

Des:
Gary, what do you think?

Gary
Lineker: I thought it was all very nice and I agree with Alan and I agree with Jimmy and I agree with you. I used to play for Barcelona, you know.

Des:
Thank you. That's all from Euro Nutty Footy. See you soon.